VirtualBox Guide for Beginners

Robert Collins

Table of Contents

Introduction

Sometimes, you may need to have a number of operating systems on your computer. In most cases, you will need to have all of these operating systems without changing how the host operating system will work. This is possible with a VirtualBox. It helps you create virtual machines with different operating systems. It is possible for you to group together your virtual machines, which will help you perform a single action such as running a command and then applying it to all the available virtual machines. It will also be possible for you to share folders between the host and the guest operating systems. This means that your guest operating system will work in a similar manner as the host operating system, with the difference being minimal. This book guides you on how to use VirtualBox. Enjoy reading!

Chapter 1- Getting Started with VirtualBox

VirtualBox is an open-source and cross-platform application used for the creation and management of virtual machines (VMs). A virtual machine refers to a computer which has its hardware components being emulated by a host computer, which is the computer running the program. You can run VirtualBox on Windows, Linux, Mac OS X, and Solaris.

With VirtualBox, you can try an operating system without having to change how your computer works. It is also good for anyone who needs to try particular software which they think is not safe. VirtualBox can provide you with adequate security. You can choose to create a virtual machine and use it for online banking and no spyware will gain access to your private data.

Installing VirtualBox

There are many different packages for VirtualBox, and the installation steps are determined by the host operating system. If you are used to installation of other types of software, then the installation of VirtualBox will be easy for you. As it is straightforward.

Installation on Windows

First, ensure that you have downloaded the VirtualBox executable onto your machine. To start the installation process, you have to double click on this installation or run the following command on the Windows command line:

VirtualBox.exe –extract

The command will extract all the installers into a temporary directory, and you will find the .MSI files here. The installation can then be done by running the command given below:

msiexec /i VirtualBox-<version>-MultiArch_<x86|amd64>.msi

This will present to you the installation dialog, and you will be prompted to choose the location in which you want to install VirtualBox. You will also have to choose the components which you need to install. Other than VortualBox, you will also be provided with the following components:

1. USB Support- this is a package with special drivers for the Windows host which VirtualBox needs so as to support USB devices fully inside the virtual machines.

2. Networking- this is a package with some extra networking drivers for the Windows host which VirtualBox needs so as to be able to support Bridge Networking. This means the

virtual network cards on your VM will be accessible from the other machines which are located on the physical network.

3. Python Support- this is a package with support for Python scripting for VirtualBox API. For this to function, you must have installed Python on your machine.

During the installation, you may be warned about "unsigned drivers" based on the kind of configuration for the Windows. Just choose "continue," as failure to do this may make VirtualBox fail later.

A VirtualBox group will then be created and installed in the Start Menu for Windows, and you will be in a position to use this for launching the application as well as accessing its documentation.

The standard setting is that the installation of the VirtualBox will be for all the users who are on your system. However, you may need to change this. In this case, you have to invoke the installer on the command line by executing the command given below:

VirtualBox.exe −extract

You can then run the following command:

VirtualBox.exe -msiparams ALLUSERS=2

Or the following:

msiexec /i VirtualBox-<version>-MultiArch_<x86|amd64>.msi ALLUSERS=2

on your .MSI files which you extracted. VirtualBox will only be installed for the current user.

Sometimes, you may not want to install all the VirtualBox features. In this case, you can use the "ADDLOCAL" parameter so as to set the features which you need to install. If you need to install the USB support as well as the other binaries, you can run the command given below:

VirtualBox.exe -msiparams ADDLOCAL=VBoxApplication,VBoxUSB

Or the following command:

msiexec /i VirtualBox-<version>-MultiArch_<x86|amd64>.msi ADDLOCAL=VBoxApplication,VBoxUSB

Installation on Mac OS X

In the case of hosts running OS X, VirtualBox comes in the form of a disk image file (dmg). The installation can be done by following the steps given below:

1. Double-click on the file so as to have the contents mounted.

2. A window will pop up instructing you to double-click the "VirtualBox.mpkg" installer file which is displayed in the window.

3. The installer will be started, and it will prompt you to choose the location in which you need to install VirtualBox.

Once the installation is complete, you will find an icon for VirtualBox in the VirtualBox folder of the Finder.

Sometimes, you may need to uninstall VirtualBox from the Mac OS X. To do this, launch your disk image file (dmg), and you will find an uninstall icon in it. Just double-click on this icon.

Installation on Linux

Before you can begin to install, you should first install the packages given below:

- Qt 4.8.0 or higher

- SDL 1.2.7 or higher

Let us discuss how one can install VirtualBox in Debian or Ubuntu. Begin by downloading the appropriate package based on the Linux distribution you are using. We are assuming that you are installing a 32-bit version of the Ubuntu wily system. The Debian package should be installed by use of "dpkg" as shown below:

sudo dpkg -i virtualbox-5.0_5.1.18_Ubuntu_wily_i386.deb

The installer will go ahead and install and build kernel modules which are good for the kernel you are currently using. In case the build process fails, then you will get a warning and the package will not be configured. You can open the "/var/log/vbox-install.log" file so as to look for the reason why the build failed.

Once you have corrected the problems, execute the following command:

sudo rcvboxdrv setup

A second attempt for building the module will then be started.

After a successful installation of VirtualBox, you can launch it by choosing "VirtualBox" from the start menu or just use the command line.

Installation on Solaris

VirtualBox comes as a standard package for Solaris. Begin by downloading the VirtualBox SunOS package which has 64-bit versions for VirtualBox. For you to do the installation, you have to be logged in as the root, as well as from the global zone since the VirtualBox installer will load the kernel drivers that are unable to be done from the non-global zones.

If you need to know the zone you are in, just run the "zonename" command. Just run the command given below:

gunzip -cd VirtualBox-5.1.18-SunOS.tar.gz | tar xvf –

You can then run the following command so as to install the VirtualBox package:

pkgadd -d VirtualBox-5.1.18-SunOS.pkg

You will be prompted by the installer so as to choose the package which you need to install. You are able to choose either 1 or "all" to proceed. You will also be prompted to choose whether you need to have your postscript script executed. This is the script responsible for execution of the installation of the VirtualBox kernel module, so it should be installed. Just type "y" for yes to install it. VirtualBox will be installed and the postscript will be executed.

The installation will be completed, and you may go ahead to delete any uncompressed package, as well as the auto response files from the system. The installation of VirtualBox will be done in the "/opt/VirtualBox" directory.

For you to start it in the easiest way, you only have to launch the package which you need to use from the terminal.

Chapter 2- Creating the First Virtual Machine

For you to be able to create a virtual machine in VirtualBox, you should first launch it. On the host with VirtualBox, click on "Applications," then "System Tools," and then "Oracle VM VirtualBox" so as to start it. You can also launch it from the terminal by running the "VirtualBox" command. You will see the Oracle VM VirtualBox displayed for you.

Note that the process of creating a virtual machine in VirtualBox can also be done via the VirtualBox command line. However, since you are a beginner, the Oracle VM VirtualBox Manger will be easier for you.

Click the "New" button from the toolbar. The wizard for creating a new Virtual Machine will pop up.

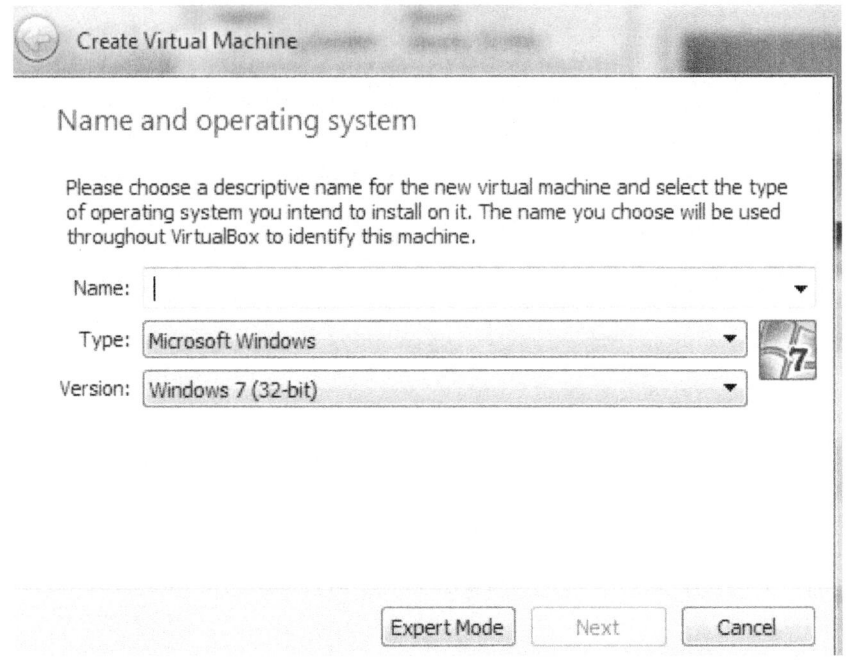

This is the wizard in which you should configure some of the basic details for your virtual machine. Type a name which will be used for describing the Virtual machine in the "Name" field, and then choose the type of the operating system as well as the version from the drop down list. Ensure that you choose the operating system correctly as well as the version, since the default settings for this will be applied. In my case, I am creating an Ubuntu 32-bit virtual machine, so I have entered the following details:

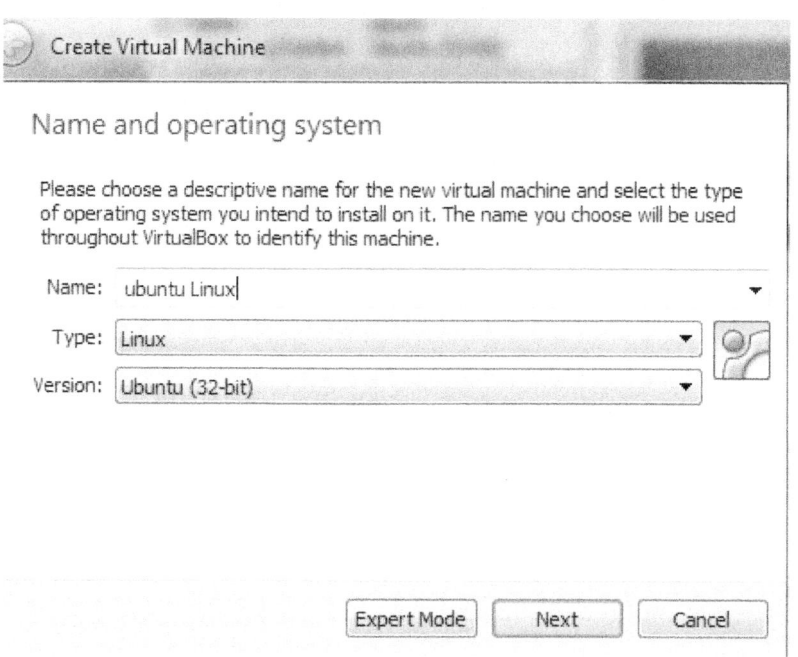

Click on "Next." You will be taken to a window for choosing the amount of memory space that you need to use. You will find a default RAM space chosen for you, so you can use the default one. Note that this can be changed later.

At this point, you should have downloaded the VDI (Virtual Disk Image) for the operating system you need to create the virtual machine for. In this step, you will find the second option selected for you, but choose the last one:

Hard disk

If you wish you can add a virtual hard disk to the new machine. You can either create a new hard disk file or select one from the list or from another location using the folder icon.

If you need a more complex storage set-up you can skip this step and make the changes to the machine settings once the machine is created.

The recommended size of the hard disk is **25.00 GB**.

○ Do not add a virtual hard disk

○ Create a virtual hard disk now

◉ Use an existing virtual hard disk file

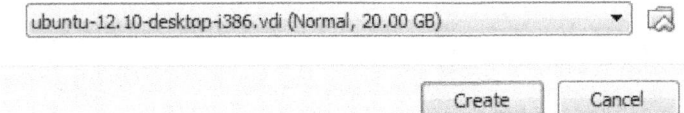

| Create | Cancel |

Click on the folder with ^ on the bottom right.

A File Dialog box will be opened, and you will be expected to choose the VDI to be used for creation of the virtual machine. In my case, I have it as shown below:

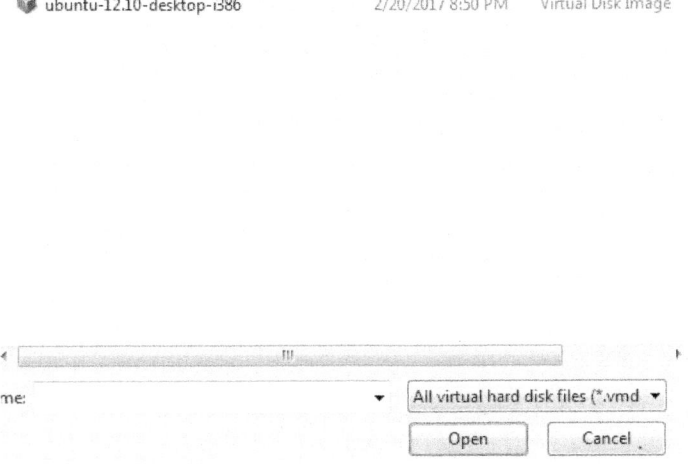

Choose your Virtual Disk Image and then click on "Create" so as to create it. After this is completed, the dialog will be closed and you will be taken back to the summary page. Your new Virtual Box Machine will then be shown in the first page.

Since you need to install the operating system in your virtual machine, it is good for you to ensure that the virtual machine is capable of accessing the installation media. For you to do this, you have to edit the settings for the virtual machine. Choose the virtual machine which you have just created, and then click on "Settings" from the toolbar. You will see a new window popup.

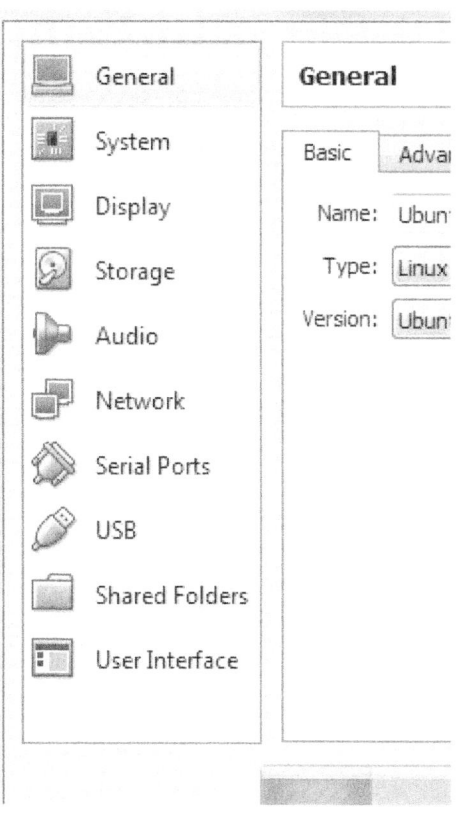

Click on Storage from the navigation pane located on the left. From the Tree section, choose "Empty," which is found below the IDE controller. You will see the attributes for the CD/DVD. Click on the CD/DVD icon, which is located near the drop-down list for CD/DVD Drive, and then select the location for your installation media as follows:

- If you need to connect a virtual CD/DVD drive to a physical CD/DVD drive of the host, choose "Host Drive *<drive-name>*."

To insert the ISO image in your virtual CD/DVD drive, choose "Choose a virtual CD/DVD disk file," and then browse for this ISO image.

Click on "Ok" so as to apply these storage settings. The window for the Settings will then be closed. If you had connected the CD/DVD drive for the virtual machine to the physical CD/DVD drive of the host, just insert your installation media in the CD/DVD drive of the host now. You can then start the virtual machine and then install your operating system.

Move back to the Oracle VM VirtualBox Manager, choose the virtual machine you have just created, and click on "Start" from the toolbar.

You will see a new window pop up, and it will show the virtual machine as it boots. Based on the operating system which you are using, the VirtualBox may show you some warnings, but just ignore them, as this is the best way to stay safe. Your virtual machine will then boot from your installation media.

You can then go ahead so as to perform all the normal steps required for the installation of an operating system. Ensure that you are able to remember the username and the password for the virtual machine which you just created, as you will need these so as to be able to log into the virtual machine. Note that as the installation process continues, the virtual machine may restart a number of times. After the installation process is completed, you can perform an update if you wish to do so.

Installation of VirtualBox Guest Additions

These are the ones with system applications and device drivers which are good for optimization of the performance of the virtual machine and increasing its usability. Automated logons is a feature which is very useful in virtual machines. For you to take advantage of this feature, you should first install the VirtualBox Guest additions in your virtual machine.

Once you have logged into the virtual machine and it is running, click on "Devices" from the toolbar, and chooses "Install Guest Additions."

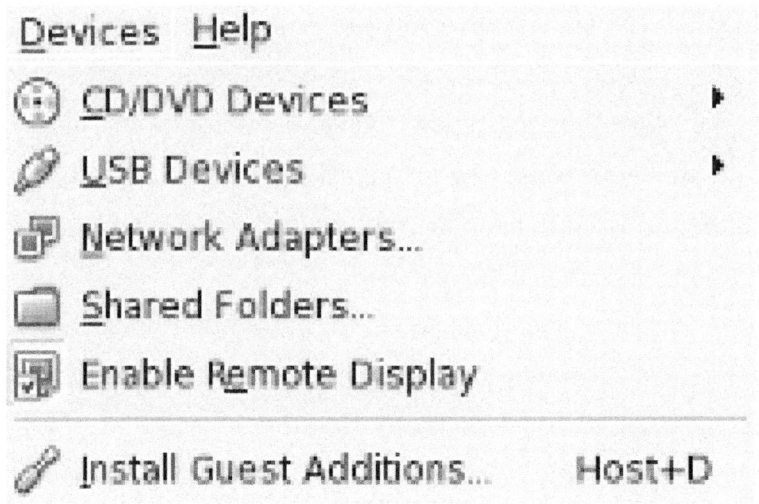

After the display of the AutoPlay window, which will prompt you to run the VBoxWindowsAdditions.exe program, just close it without the guest additions. When the window is closed, the ISO image will be left used to install Guest Additions inserted into a virtual CD/DVD drive. The VirtualBox Guest Additions should be installed from the command line so that we may get all the features which are necessary for us. This will then guide you through all the necessary steps for you to install the Guest Additions, so you only have to follow.

Chapter 3- Creating a Hadoop Cluster

It is possible for us to create a Hadoop cluster in VirtualBox. You should have the virtual machine created, and configured with all the necessary parameters and settings so that it can work like a cluster node. The referenced virtual machine will be cloned many times since the Hadoop cluster will have nodes.

We will be using the CentOS Linux distribution.

VM Creation

Begin by creating a reference virtual machine with the configurations given below:

- Bridge network

- Enough disk space (over 40GB)

- 2 GB of RAM

- Setup the DVD to point to your CentOS ISO image

After installation of CentOS, just specify the "expert text" option to facilitate a faster installation of the OS with the minimum set of the packages.

Network Configuration

We need to have the nodes contained in the cluster able to communicate with each other. This calls for us to make some network configurations which will help us to achieve this. Setup the following changes in the files given below:

/etc/resolv.conf:

This file should have the following contents:

search example.com

nameserver 10.0.1.1

Note that to edit the contents of the file, you have to open it in your editor, such as the Vi editor.

The file will then be opened in your editor.

You can then edit the following file:

/etc/sysconfig/network:

The file should have the contents given below:

NETWORKING=yes

HOSTNAME=base.example.com
GATEWAY=10.0.1.1

Next is the following file:

/etc/sysconfig/network-scripts/ifcfg-eth0:

Edit it to have the following contents:

DEVICE=eth0
ONBOOT=yes
PROTO=static
IPADDR=10.0.1.200
NETMASK=255.255.255.0

Next open the following file:

/ETC/SELINUX/CONFIG

Edit its contents to the following:

SELINUX=disabled

Next edit the following file:

/etc/yum/pluginconf.d/fastestmirror.conf

To have the following:

enabled=0

We should now apply the changes by restarting the network services. You can run the following commands:

$> chkconfig iptables off
$> /etc/init.d/network restart

The networking services will be restarted and the changes will take effect.

Installing VM Additions

At this point, you should update all the available packages and then reboot your virtual machine. First, update the packages by running the following command:

$> yum update

Next, run the following command to reboot your virtual machine:

$> reboot

Choose "Devices," and then "Insert Guest..." from the VirtualBox menu. This will insert the DVD with the ISO image of your guest additions in your DVD player of the VM. You can then run the following commands so as to mount the DVD and be able to access the DVD:

```
$> mkdir /media/VBGuest
$> mount -r /dev/cdrom /media/VBGuest
```

Setting up the Cluster Hosts

For us to have an easy access, all our hosts should be defined in the "/etc/hosts" file for those who have no DNS setup in which the definition of this can be done. If you need to have more nodes in the cluster, you should add extra clusters. Consider the following file with my hosts:

/ETC/HOSTS:
```
10.0.1.205 hadoop1.example.com hadoop1
10.0.1.205 hadoop2.example.com hadoop2
10.0.1.205 hadoop3.example.com hadoop3
10.0.1.205 hadoop4.example.com hadoop4
```

SSH Setup

To make it simple for access between hosts, we have to install and then setup the SSH keys, and then define them as it has been authorized. The following set of commands can help us achieve this:

```
$> yum -y install perl openssh-clients
$> ssh-keygen (press enter, enter, enter)
$> cd ~/.ssh
$> cp id_rsa.pub authorized_keys
```

You should then modify your SSH configuration file. We don't need to be asked any question when we are establishing a connection to the SSH. This calls for us to uncomment this and set its value to "no":

/ETC/SSH/SSH_CONFIG:

THIS IS THE LINE:

StrictHostKeyChecking no

Now, run the following command so as to shutdown the system:

$> init 0

We can now create server nodes which will act as the members of the cluster.

The base server should be cloned in the VirtualBox by use of the "Linked Clone" option then name hadoop1, hadoop2, hadoop3, and hadoop4 nodes.

The size of memory for the first node (hadoop1) should be changed to 80GB, as it is the node which most of the roles will be installed, and it must have enough memory available for this.

Clones Customization

Carry out the operations given below in each of your notes:

Change the server hostname by changing the "/etc/sysconfig/network" file to have the following code:

HOSTNAME=hadoop[n].example.com

Whereby the n represents the number for nodes and it ranges from 1 to 4. The fixed IP address of the server should also be changed by modifying the line given below in the "/etc/sysconfig/network-scripts/ifcfg-eth0" file:

IPADDR=10.0.1.20[n]

Whereby n represents the number of nodes and it should take values from 1 to 4. We can then launch our networking services, and then reboot the server, and the changes will take effect:

$> /etc/init.d/network restart
$> init 6

After that, you will have four virtual machines running with a correct configuration of the CentOS.

Installing Cloudera Manager on hadoop1

Begin by downloading and running the Cloudera Manager Installer. This tool will make it easy for you to do the rest of the work:

$> curl -O https://archive.cloudera.com/cm5/installer/latest/cloudera-manager-installer.bin

$> chmod +x cloudera-manager-installer.bin
$> ./cloudera-manager-installer.bin

You can open your browser, and then open the **http://hadoop1.example.com:7180** URL. For those who had not added hostnames to the hosts file or DNS, use the **http://10.0.1.201:7180** URL.

For you to proceed with the installation, you will have to choose the Cloudera free license version. The nodes to be used in your cluster will also have to be defined. Type in all the nodes which you had created in our previous steps and use a space to separate them. Once done, click on the "Search" button. You can make use of the generated SSH keys or the root password so as to automate connectivity between different nodes. All the services and packages should be installed in our first node, which is hadoop1.

After the completion of this, you will have to choose additional service components. Select everything as by default. You will see the installation process continue until completed.

The Hadoop cluster will now be ready for use. It will provide you with two clusters which you will be in a position to use so as to operate your cluster. These include the Hue and the Cloud Manager.

Cloudera Manager

Launch your browser and open the
http://hadoop1.example.com:7180 URL.

If you had not added the hostnames to hosts file or DNS, use the
http://10.0.1.201:7180 URL.

Hue

Also, to the Cloudera Manager, it is possible for you to access the Hue administration site by use of the following URL:

http://hadoop1.example.com:8888

This will permit you to access the different services which you installed into the cluster.

Chapter 4- Creating and Managing VM Groups

You might have or use many virtual machines in your VirtualBox. In such a case, you should create a "VM Group." It can help you to place or categorize your virtual machines into groups, making it easy for you to work and manage them. We will be showing you how to create and manage a VM group.

When you create many VM groups, the management of your virtual machines will become easier. It will allow you to apply a single action to a number of virtual machines. A good example of such an action is a command, which can be executed on all the machines you have in your VM group. Note that this action will be applied at the same time. Suppose you have a VM group with Linux virtual machines. You can use just a single click so as to startup all of these virtual machines.

There are a number of ways that you can create a VM group in Virtualbox. You can use the command prompt or the VirtualBox manager GUI. The easiest steps for you to create a VM group are outlined below:

1. Select the Virtual Machines which you need to create the VM group for. To do this, you just have to click on the first one, and then hold down your Ctrl key as you click on the others. It will be possible for you to add the other virtual machines to the group by drag and drop if you need to do so.

2. Now that you have selected the virtual machines, right click on the selection, and then choose "Group."

   If you need to rename your group, just right click on the title bar for the group, and then choose the option for "Rename Group." You can also simply click on the F2 key.

That is how you can create your VM group via the GUI. It is also possible for you to create your VM group via the command prompt.

Group membership is simply an attribute of a VM, meaning that it is possible for you to modify a VM so as to belong to a group. Suppose you have a virtual machine named "Ubuntu" and you need to add it to a group named "VMGroup," just run the command given below:

VBoxManage modifyvm "Ubuntu" --groups "/VMGroup"

Also, it is good for you to be aware that a single virtual machine can be made to belong to more than one VM group.

When you are dragging your virtual machine from one VM group to another, you should ensure that it will belong to both of these groups. You only have to hold down the Alt key and this will ensure that this remains. You can run the following command on the command prompt:

VBoxManage modifyvm "Ubuntu" --groups "/VMGroup","/ProjectX","/ProjectY"

In the above command, your "Ubuntu" virtual machine will belong to all the groups which you have specified. Sometimes, you may need to view all the virtual machines which are available in a particular VM group. To do this, just press the right/left arrow which is located at the top of the VM group. To exit the group or go back to the page with all the virtual machines, just press the left arrow.

When you keep your virtual machine in a VM group, it will be easy for you to have an organized GUI. Again, it will make it easy and faster for you to carry out tasks on the virtual machines, as it will be possible for you to do a single action in all virtual machines contained in the group in a single click. A good example is powering on of all the virtual machines at once.

At the VM group level, you can perform starts, which can be from any state, such as boot or resume. You can also start your virtual machines in a headless mode by holding down the Shift key as they start. You can also Pause, Close, Save state, Reset, Send Shutdown signal, Discard saved state, Power off, Show in the file system, and Sort the virtual machines in the VM group.

Removing a VM Group

Sometimes, you may need to remove a VM group. To do this, you only have to right click on the group, and then choose "Ungroup". Once you do this, your virtual machines will be placed in their normal places in your GUI.

Also, sometimes you may only want to remove a particular virtual machine from a particular VM group. This can simply be done by dragging the virtual machine from the VM group and then placing it in an empty space within the console. Avoid selecting to remove the virtual machine, as this will remove it completely from the host. That is how you can remove it from the VM group via the GUI.

However, it is possible for you to achieve the same from the command prompt. This can be done by running the following command on the command prompt:

VBoxManage modifyvm "Ubuntu" --groups ""

What we have done in the above command is that we have specified the virtual machine which we need to remove from the group, and in the case of the group, we have specified it as empty (""). This means that it will not belong to any VM group.

Chapter 5- Emulating a Network in VirtualBox

It is possible for you to use the graphical user interface of VirtualBox so as to create a network of devices. In this case, we will be setting up a network of three devices which include three PCs and three routers. We will be using the advanced features provided by VirtualBox to emulate a network of devices.

You should have some basic understanding of the Linux shell commands. Before we can begin, come out with a layout plan for your network which you will be creating. However, VirtualBox will not provide you with a drag and drop user interface for you to create the network components. This means that for you to draw in this case, you will have to use tools such as Microsoft Powerpoint, LibreOffice Draw, or Dia as well as other basic tools such as a pencil and paper.

First, determine the ports which you will connect to which networks before you can begin the creation of the virtual machines. Plan on how the emulated nodes will be managed. You can then come up with a configuration plan for your network. You only have to create a small network made up of three routers and three PCs, in which each router will be connected to a PC.

VirtualBox Network Topology

This topology is made up of the virtual machines which are an interconnected host computer as well as the external networks which we can reach from our host computer. The connection between a virtual machine to the other virtual machines will be done by the internal networks for VirtualBox. Add a network adapter to every guest VM, and then attach it to the VirtualBox NAT interface so as to connect every guest VM to the host computer as well as to the external networks.

The base VM

For you to be able to create a network topology, you must first create a new VM. We will be using an Ubuntu Server 16.04 as the base VM in this case. The default configurations will be used. The hostname is "ubuntu," which is the default. It will be good for you to use this name; otherwise, there are some modifications you will have to do in our commands.

Cloning Virtual Machines

If you need to have many more guest virtual machines on your computer, just clone the virtual machine. For us to create the routers and PCs for emulation of our network, we will have to clone the Ubuntu Server VM which we had created. Right click on this VM, and the choose "Clone."

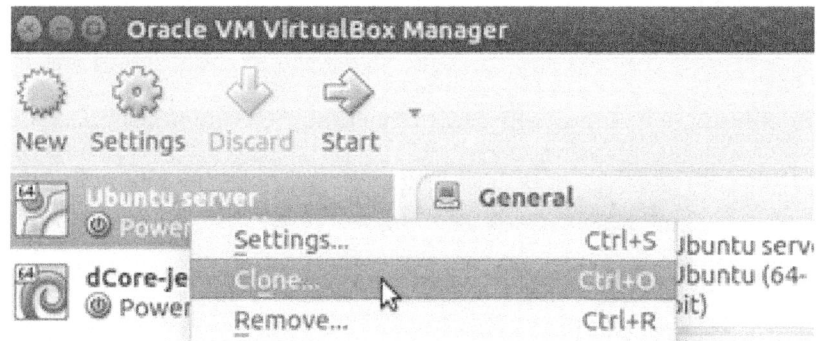

You will see a new box popup after this. You can type in the name for your VM. Ensure that the checkbox for the "Reinitialize the MAC address of all network cards" is activated. The MAC addresses for the VM machines which have been cloned should be different.

In your next dialogue box, just choose a "Linked clone." This is a good feature which will ensure that the clones maintain a very small size.

If you choose **Linked clone**, a new machine will be created, but the virtual hard disk files will be tied to the virtual hard disk files of original machine and you will not be able to move the new virtual machine to a different computer without moving the original as well.

If you create a **Linked clone** then a new snapshot will be created in the original virtual machine as part of the cloning process.

○ Full clone

● Linked clone

| < Back | Clone | Cancel |

Finally, click on the "Clone" button, and you will see the clone appear in the manager window for the VirtualBox. You can then repeat similar steps for all the virtual machines which we want to use. You should create six virtual machines and ensure that all of these are linked to the Ubuntu server VM which had created. The virtual machines names should be chosen so that they can match the ones you have on the network diagram.

You will then have six virtual machines. Each of these VMs should be setup so as to have network interfaces connected to the internal networks for VirtualBox.

Creating the Internal Networks

The graphical user interface for VirtualBox supports four network adapters only for each virtual machine. This is good so as to prevent your network from become too complex for management.

You may enable or disable each of these network adapters. If you enable any of these, you will be in a position to use it for connection to the interfaces which are provided by VirtualBox. If you need to connect any of the available virtual machines together, just use the Internal Network interface.

From the window of your VirtualBox Manager, select of any of the available virtual machines, and then click the Settings option from the toolbar. A window will appear, so click on "Network.".

Activate the check box for "Enable Network Adapter," click the "Attached Network," and then choose "Internal Network."

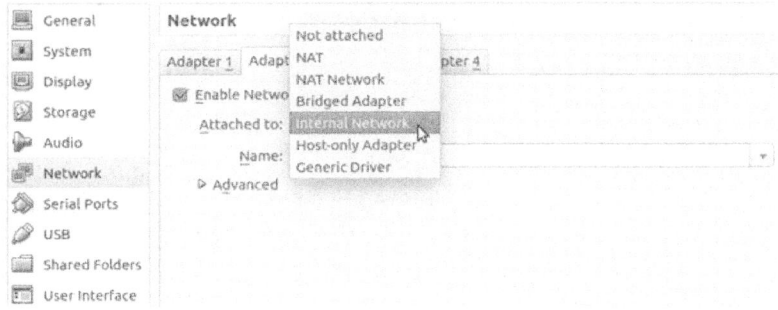

You can then give a name to the internal network. Ensure that you use the name you had used to configure the network adapter which corresponds to this on the VM which you need to connect to this.

Do the same for each node. Each router will use the three or the four available network adapters so as to connect to the internal networks. Each PC will use one network adapter so as to connect to the internal networks.

Port Forwarding

We now need to configure port forwarding on each of our NAT interfaces.

Select settings on each virtual machine, and then click the "Network" tab in the window which pops up. Choose the "Adapter 1" tab. Advance the network panel for "Advanced," and then click "Port Forwarding."

You will see a new window for the Port Forwarding Rules. This is shown below:

Click on the green button with a plus (+) symbol so that you may add a new rule. Type is in a name for the rule. Use any name that you want, but in my case, I have used "SSH" as the name, and the protocol should be TCP. The Guest Port should be 22. The host port refers to any TCP port which you have in your computer. In this case, we will use port 14601.

Name	Protocol	Host IP	Host Port	Guest IP	Guest Port
SSH	TCP		14601		22

Repeat similar steps so as to setup NAT interfaces having port forwarding rules for every interface. For me to connect to the virtual node from my computer, I will have to use the IP address of the loopback interface of our host computer and the TCP port number of the host. It is impossible for you to use the IP address of the virtual machine, since it is hidden behind a NAT firewall.

Now, it is a good time for you to start the virtual machines. It is good for you to create a way that you will identify the virtual machines which you have created for emulation purposes. In VirtualBox, it is possible for you to group together your virtual machines. It will be good for you to group all the virtual machines which you had created for simulation of the network so that you will be able to start them at once and be able to differentiate them from the other virtual machines found in your VirtualBox GUI. You can then select your group and click on the green button so as to launch the network emulation.

Connecting to the Virtual Machines

Now that you have started the virtual machines, you can use SSH so as to log into them. Some minutes will elapse before they can run. You should use the IP address of the host machine and the port number which was assigned to the virtual machine. The following command can help you to do the login:

$ ssh -l <userid> -p <port number> <IP address>

The use of the –l option helps us to specify the userid for logging into the node. The –p option helps us specify the port number on the host. The TCP port is now listening for the host computer to forward traffic to the port number 22 which is associated with the virtual machine.

Network Configuration

We should now configure our network interfaces on the virtual machines. The routers should also be installed with the routing software as well as the routing protocols. Let us guide you on how to do the configurations for each PC:

PC-1

You have to change its hostname, add an interface configuration to your network interfaces file, and then add a static route. Run the following command:

sudo su

Type in your password, and paste the commands given below on the terminals:

bash <<EOF2
sed -i 's/ubuntu/pc1/g' /etc/hostname
sed -i 's/ubuntu/pc1/g' /etc/hosts
hostname pc1
cat >> /etc/network/interfaces << EOF

auto enpos8

iface enpos8 inet static

 address 192.168.1.1

 netmask 255.255.255.0

up route add -net 192.168.0.0/16 gw 192.168.1.254 dev enpos8

EOF

/etc/init.d/networking restart

Exit

EOF2

You can then run the following command so as to reboot the node:

sudo reboot

You can then use SSH so as to log back into your node from your host computer. You just have to run the SSH command given below:

ssh -l nicohsam -p 14501 localhost

PC-2

You have to change its hostname, add an interface configuration to your network interfaces file, and then add a static route. Run the following command:

sudo su

Type in the password and paste the following set of commands on the terminal. Note that you should run the commands one by one:

```
bash <<EOF2
sed -i 's/ubuntu/pc2/g' /etc/hostname
sed -i 's/ubuntu/pc2/g' /etc/hosts
hostname pc2
cat >> /etc/network/interfaces << EOF
auto enpos8
iface enpos8 inet static
  address 192.168.2.1
  netmask 255.255.255.0

up route add -net 192.168.0.0/16 gw 192.168.2.254 dev enpos8
```

EOF

/etc/init.d/networking restart
Exit

EOF2

Run the following command so as to reboot the node:

sudo reboot

You can then log back into the node from the host computer by running the following SSH command:

ssh -l nicohsam -p 14502 localhost

Note that "nicohsam" is my username, so make sure that you use your right username.

PC-3

You have to change its hostname, add an interface configuration to your network interfaces file, and then add a static route. Run the following command:

sudo su

Type in the password and paste the following set of commands on the terminal. Note that you should run the commands one by one:

bash <<EOF2
sed -i 's/ubuntu/pc3/g' /etc/hostname
sed -i 's/ubuntu/pc3/g' /etc/hosts
hostname pc3
cat >> /etc/network/interfaces << EOF
auto enpos8
iface enpos8 inet static
address 192.168.3.1
netmask 255.255.255.0
up route add -net 192.168.0.0/16 gw 192.168.3.254 dev enpos8

EOF

/etc/init.d/networking restart

Exit

EOF2

Reboot the node by running the following command:

sudo reboot

You can then run the following command so as to log back into the node from the host command via SSH:

ssh -l nicohsam -p 14503 localhost

Router-1

In this router, you have to change its hostname, install quagga, and then configure OSPF on the interfaces of the router. Run the following command first:

sudo su

You can type in the password, and then paste the commands given below in the terminal of the window:

bash <<EOF2

sed -i 's/ubuntu/router1/g' /etc/hostname

sed -i 's/ubuntu/router1/g' /etc/hosts

```
hostname router1
apt-get update
apt-get install quagga quagga-doc traceroute

cp /usr/share/doc/quagga/examples/zebra.conf.sample
/etc/quagga/zebra.conf

cp /usr/share/doc/quagga/examples/ospfd.conf.sample
/etc/quagga/ospfd.conf

chown quagga.quaggavty /etc/quagga/*.conf
chmod 640 /etc/quagga/*.conf
sed -i s'/zebra=no/zebra=yes/' /etc/quagga/daemons
sed -i s'/ospfd=no/ospfd=yes/' /etc/quagga/daemons
echo 'VTYSH_PAGER=more' >>/etc/environment
echo 'export VTYSH_PAGER=more' >>/etc/bash.bashrc
cat >> /etc/quagga/ospfd.conf << EOF
interface enpos8
interface enpos9
interface enpos10
interface lo
router ospf
 passive-interface enpos8
 network 192.168.1.0/24 area 0.0.0.0
 network 192.168.100.0/24 area 0.0.0.0
 network 192.168.101.0/24 area 0.0.0.0
line vty
EOF

cat >> /etc/quagga/zebra.conf << EOF
```

```
interface enpos8
 ip address 192.168.1.254/24
 ipv6 nd suppress-ra
interface enpos9
 ip address 192.168.100.1/24
 ipv6 nd suppress-ra
interface enpos10
 ip address 192.168.101.2/24
 ipv6 nd suppress-ra
interface lo
ip forwarding
line vty
EOF
/etc/init.d/quagga start
Exit
```

EOF2

Run the following command so as to restart the node:

sudo reboot

Use SSH to log back into your host computer, and then execute the SSH command given below:

ssh -l nicohsam -p 14601 localhost

Router-2

In this router, you have to change its hostname, install quagga, and then configure OSPF on the interfaces of the router. Run the following command first:

sudo su

You can type in the password, and then paste the commands given below in the terminal of the window:

bash <<EOF2
sed -i 's/ubuntu/router2/g' /etc/hostname
sed -i 's/ubuntu/router2/g' /etc/hosts
hostname router2
apt-get update
apt-get install quagga quagga-doc traceroute

cp /usr/share/doc/quagga/examples/zebra.conf.sample /etc/quagga/zebra.conf

cp /usr/share/doc/quagga/examples/ospfd.conf.sample /etc/quagga/ospfd.conf

chown quagga.quaggavty /etc/quagga/*.conf
chmod 640 /etc/quagga/*.conf
sed -i s'/zebra=no/zebra=yes/' /etc/quagga/daemons
sed -i s'/ospfd=no/ospfd=yes/' /etc/quagga/daemons
echo 'VTYSH_PAGER=more' >>/etc/environment
echo 'export VTYSH_PAGER=more' >>/etc/bash.bashrc

```
cat >> /etc/quagga/ospfd.conf << EOF
interface enpos8
interface enpos9
interface enpos10
interface lo
router ospf
 passive-interface enpos8
 network 192.168.2.0/24 area 0.0.0.0
 network 192.168.100.0/24 area 0.0.0.0
 network 192.168.102.0/24 area 0.0.0.0
 line vty
EOF
cat > /etc/quagga/zebra.conf << EOF
interface enpos8
 ip address 192.168.2.254/24
 ipv6 nd suppress-ra
interface enpos9
 ip address 192.168.100.2/24
 ipv6 nd suppress-ra
interface enpos10
 ip address 192.168.102.2/24
 ipv6 nd suppress-ra
interface lo
ip forwarding
line vty
```

EOF

/etc/init.d/quagga start

Exit

EOF2

Run the following command to reboot your node:

sudo reboot

Run the following SSH command when logged into the host computer:

ssh –l nicohsam -p 14602 localhost

Router-3

Run the following command:

sudo su

Paste the following commands on the terminal window:

bash <<EOF2
sed -i 's/ubuntu/router3/g' /etc/hostname
sed -i 's/ubuntu/router3/g' /etc/hosts
hostname router3
apt-get update

```
apt-get install quagga quagga-doc traceroute
cp /usr/share/doc/quagga/examples/zebra.conf.sample
/etc/quagga/zebra.conf

cp /usr/share/doc/quagga/examples/ospfd.conf.sample
/etc/quagga/ospfd.conf

chown quagga.quaggavty /etc/quagga/*.conf
chmod 640 /etc/quagga/*.conf
sed -i s'/zebra=no/zebra=yes/' /etc/quagga/daemons
sed -i s'/ospfd=no/ospfd=yes/' /etc/quagga/daemons
echo 'VTYSH_PAGER=more' >>/etc/environment
echo 'export VTYSH_PAGER=more' >>/etc/bash.bashrc
cat >> /etc/quagga/ospfd.conf << EOF
interface enpos8
interface enpos9
interface enpos10
interface lo
router ospf
 passive-interface enpos8
 network 192.168.3.0/24 area 0.0.0.0
 network 192.168.101.0/24 area 0.0.0.0
 network 192.168.102.0/24 area 0.0.0.0
line vty
EOF
cat > /etc/quagga/zebra.conf << EOF
interface enpos8
 ip address 192.168.3.254/24
 ipv6 nd suppress-ra
interface enpos9
```

```
ip address 192.168.101.1/24
ipv6 nd suppress-ra
interface enpos10
ip address 192.168.102.1/24
ipv6 nd suppress-ra
interface lo
ip forwarding
line vty
EOF
/etc/init.d/quagga start
Exit
```

EOF2

Run the command given below to reboot the node:

sudo reboot

Execute the following command from the host computer:

ssh -l nicohsam -p 14603 localhost

Testing the Network

If we have everything set correctly, we should have our virtual PCs and routers in our emulated network being able to communicate with each virtual PC as well as the routers you have in the network.

You can perform some experiments so as to be certain of these. Use tools such as "ping" and "tracert" to test for connectivity and how the packets are flowing in our network.

Chapter 6- Installing VirtualBox Extension Pack

Sometimes, once you plug a USB flash drive into VirtualBox running a Windows virtual machine, you may get the "This device cannot start. (Code 10)" error. For you to solve this problem, you should install the "VirtualBox Extension Pack." The ability of VirtualBox to support the use of USB is very essential, but it is unfortunate that it doesn't support it by default. The easiest solution to this problem is by installing the extension pack.

Begin by downloading the VirtualBox Extension Pack into the host operating system. Launch your VirtualBox, click "File," and then click on "Preferences."

The Preferences window will pop up. Find the "Extensions" options on its left hand side and click on it. Identify the icon located on the right hand side, and click on it so as to add a new extension (⬦).

A file dialog will appear, so browse to the folder in which you have stored the guest addition you have just downloaded. Select it, and then click on "Open" so as to add to your virtual machine. Click on the "Install" button, read all the license agreements, and then proceed with the installation process.

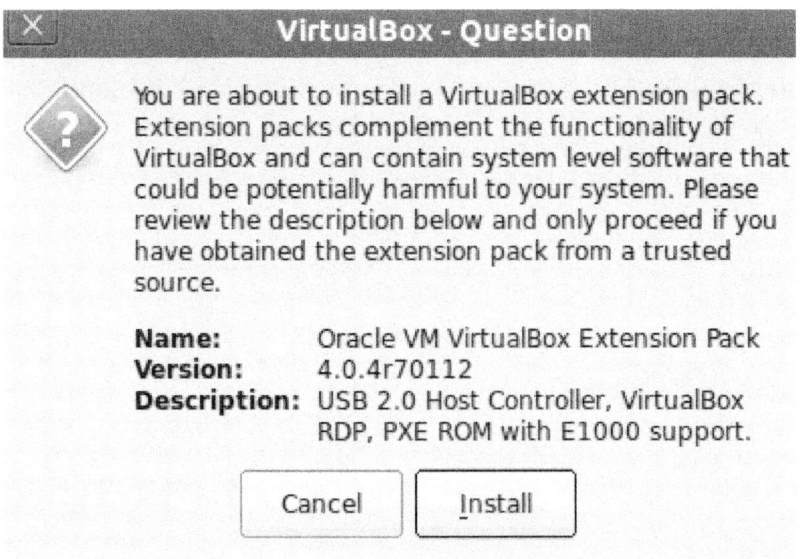

The installation of the VirtualBox Extension Pack will be done. You can click "Ok" so as to finish.

You can then restart your Virtual machine and open the Computer Section. You will have the chance to access all the USB devices from there.

Chapter 7- Sharing Folders between Host and Guest in VirtualBox

For organizations in which VirtualBox is used in the data centers, there come times in which there is a need to move a folder from the host to the guest or vice versa. Most people will opt to use third party solutions such as DropBox, which is not very effective. You can do it from within.

For you to be able to share the files, you should begin by installing the Guest Additions. This will help the guest be able to recognize the vboxsf file system so as to be able to share the folders. We discussed how the installation of Guest Additions can be done in our previous chapters, so consult from there.

Once the installation has been completed, just run the following command so as to add the user to vboxsf group:

sudo usermod -aG vboxsf $(whoami)

You should now be aware of the location of the folder which is to be shared on the host machine. Suppose you are using a Linux host operating system and you need to use the "~/Public" folder, the host will be able to see then use this folder.

Once you have booted the guest, click on Devices -> Shared Folders -> Shared Folder Settings. A window will pop up, and it is here that you will have to create a transient folder. Click on the + button, and then choose Folder Path from the provided drop-down.

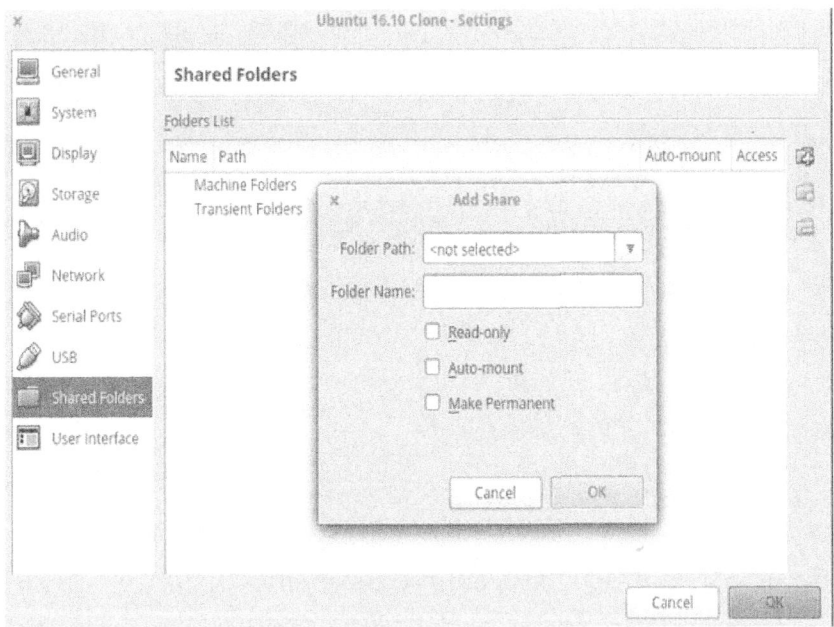

From this drop-down, choose "Other," and then navigate to choose the folder from the host. In my case, this is the "~/Public" folder. In the field for "Folder Name," type "Public" as the folder name. You can also use any other name which you need for the shared folder to show on the guest. Enable Auto-mount, and then click "Ok."

On the window for VirtualBox settings, click on Ok and you will have setup the shared folder.

Mounting a Shared Folder

This should be done from the guest. Assuming you are using a guest of the Linux type, follow the steps given below:

1. Launch the terminal window.

2. Run the "sudo mount -t vboxsf Public ~/Public" command so as to mount your shared folder.

3. Open the file manager and the contents of "~/Public" will be seen in the folder.

Since you activated auto mount when creating the shared folder, it will be mounted automatically during boot time. Since your user was added to vboxsf group, you will be in a position to access your shared folder without having to change the permissions. At this point, you are able to share your folders between the VirtualBox guest and the host. The same process will have to be done for all of the other guests, but note that after setting them up, you will be granted full access to the shared folder.

Chapter 8- Adding a New Drive to Virtual Machines

To add a disk, follow the steps given below:

1. Add your actual disk. It will be another virtual disk (meaning you are not adding a physical drive to the VM).

2. Power down your VM. (Do not save the state but let it be powered down),

3. Select it in the VirtualBox main window, and then click Settings.

4. From the Settings window, click on the Storage section.

5. Under Storage tree, click the Controller: SATA then, near bottom, click on Add Disk button, and then select Add Hard Disk.

6. In the new window, click on Create New Disk, and then walk through the Create Virtual Hard Disk wizard: Choose VDI, either Dynamically Allocated or a Fixed Size, Name, and th size of the disk (if dynamic), and then click Create. You should have a new, unformatted drive already attached to the VM

7. Click on OK so as to close out the Settings window, and then fire up the VM.

After you start up the VM, it should automatically detect the new drive. This will be shown as unformatted, meaning that it is not ready for use. The method you use to format this will be determined by the platform you are using. Let us demonstrate how you can do this using Ubuntu 16.10. Launch the Disks Tool, which should be the GNOME Disks.

Click on the Gear icon, located below Volumes, choose Format Partition, select what you need, give a name to the drive, and then click on Format. If you are asked, just click to format for the second time and your drive will be made ready for your use.

Conclusion

We have come to the end of this guide. You are now aware of how to accomplish most of the tasks in VirtualBox. With VirtualBox, you can have more operating systems and other applications installed on your computer without changing how your computer works. It is the best solution if you need to run as many operating systems as possible on your computer. Your host operating system will be left untouched, and you will continue to use other operating systems. The good thing with VirtualBox is that it can run on Windows, Linux, Mac OS X, and Solaris platforms. You only have to download the right version based on the operating system you are using, and then install it. You can also use it to create virtual machines for the different operating systems.

Printed in Great Britain
by Amazon

78002835R00037